Published by Old Stone Press an imprint of J. H. Clark & Associates, Inc
520 Old Stone Lane, Louisville KY 40207
www.oldstonepress.com

Essay: Hillary Sullivan
Essay: Lois Dodd
Artists Statements: Sally Hazelet Drummond
Book design: Izzy Cable
Photographs: Alexandre Gallery; Jessica Kincaid

For information about special discounts for bulk purchases or autographed copies
of this catalogue, please contact Old Stone Press at (502) 693-1506 or the curator,
Hillary Sullivan at hillary.sullivan@aol.com

This catalogue is published on the occasion of exhibition

Iconoclastic Fervor: Sally Hazelet Drummond's Road to Abstraction
November 19 through December 18, 2015
Hite Art Institute
University of Louisville
Louisville, Kentucky

ISBN: 978-1-938462-21-4
Library of Congress Control Number: 2015917094

Published in the USA

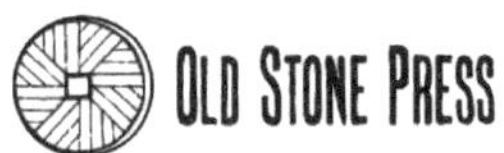

Iconoclastic Fervor:

Sally Hazelet Drummond's
Road to Abstraction

This exhibition and accompanying catalogue would not have
been possible without the generous support of the University
of Louisville's Hite Art Institute. *Iconoclastic Fervor: Sally Hazelet
Drummond's Road to Abstraction* was curated by Hillary Sullivan in
partial fulfillment for her master's degree in Critical and Curatorial
Studies from the University of Louisville. Peter Morrin and John
Begley were invaluable resources in refining the content of this
catalogue. Lois Dodd contributed the essay on Sally Hazelet
Drummond. Zaurie Zimmerman provided permission to reprint
a "World of Silent Painting" on behalf of her late father and *Arts
in Louisville Magazine* editor Leo Zimmerman. Leslie Friesen and
Izzy Cable provided the guidance and creative vision for the
design of the catalogue. Jessica Kincaid supplied photography and
exhibition installation support. John H. Clark, the artist's nephew,
and owner of Old Stone Press was instrumental in publishing this
volume and was a generous lender. I am also indebted to other
lenders, Craig W. Clark, Sally Hazelet Drummond's niece, and
Alexandre Gallery which lent many of the works in the exhibition
and provided photographs. In particular, I would like to thank
Marie Evans, Julia Benjamin, Maria Stabio and Phil Alexandre
from Alexandre Gallery.

*A special thanks is also due to Sally Hazelet Drummond and
Craig Drummond for all of their involvement and support.*

- Hillary Sullivan
 Curator

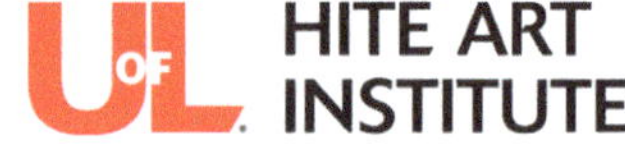

Contents

Essays

    Sally Hazelet Drummond's Iconoclastic Spirit 12

    A Conversation with Lois Dodd about Sally Hazelet Drummond 20

    An Interview with the Artist 22

Selected Artist's Statements

    Simple Abstraction 33

    World of Silent Painting 34

    Great Art 36

    Gallery Talk 38

Catalogue of Exhibited Works 47

Artist's CV 76

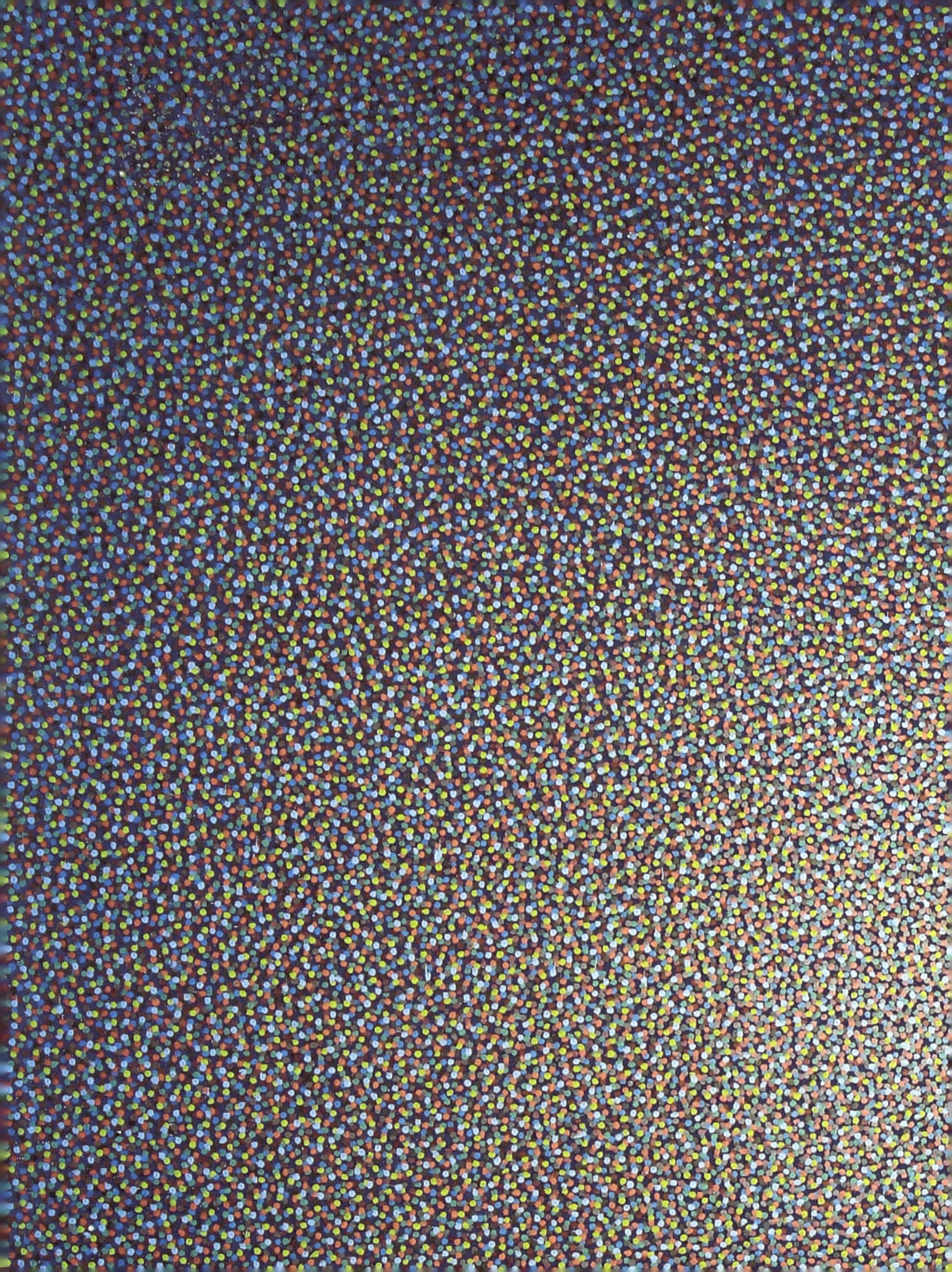

Essays

*The following is a series of essays written for the exhibition **Iconoclastic Fervor: Sally Hazelet Drummond's Road to Abstraction**. Included in this section is the curatorial essay, a conversation about Drummond by fellow Tanager Gallery member, Lois Dodd and an interview conducted with the artist at her residence in Germantown, New York.*

Previous page: Detail of *Unified Field*, 1980, Oil on Canvas, 30″ x 30″, © Sally Hazelet Drummond, courtesy Alexandre Gallery, New York

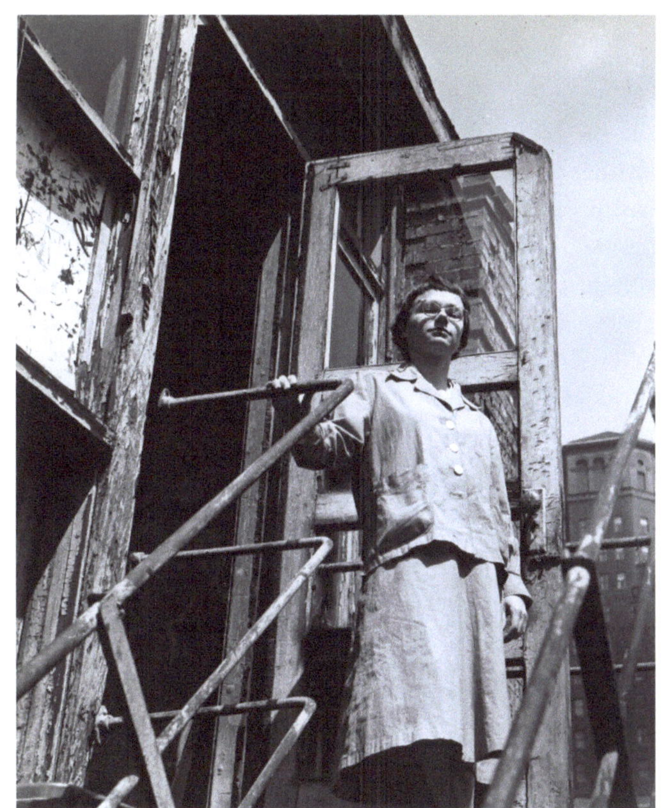

Sally Hazelet Drummond
10th Street
New York, New York
c. 1955
Photographer unkown

Sally Hazelet Drummond's Iconoclastic Spirit

This exhibition is a celebration of the art and life of Sally Hazelet Drummond. It also illustrates how Abstract Expressionism is an ideology as well as an historical art movement. The exhibition demonstrates how Drummond evolved beyond this artistic style into a method of working that prefigures many important developments in the latter 20th century.

Preface

Abstract Expressionism is an art movement that flourished between 1945-1962. Since Sally Hazelet Drummond lived and worked in New York following her graduate studies at the University of Louisville, the focus of this discussion is primarily on the movement in New York, however there were corollary iterations, such as West Coast Abstract Expressionism, that also presented methods of artmaking that are similar to Drummond's development of alternatives to the standard individualistic expressionism usually associated with the style. Drawing inspiration out of previous art movements, namely Cubism, Surrealism, and German Expressionism, the movement combined Existentialist and Freudian philosophy to push the boundaries of modern art. Considered to be the first major American contribution to art history, Abstract Expressionism also marks the rise of the art critic. More than ever before, the opinions of art critics were sought out and listened to by the artists, the art establishment and the general public. Chief among these critics was Clement Greenberg, who was the first to exalt the movement and champion artists such as Jackson Pollock and Willem de Kooning, but other important writers included Harold Rosenberg, Thomas Hess, Barbara Rose and Irving Sandler.[1]

What is now known as Abstract Expressionism was at the time known by several different titles: Action Painting,[2] American-Type,[3] Abstract-Individualism,[4] to name a few, which demonstrates the multiplicity of understandings about what exactly constituted the new movement.

1. Greenberg, Clement .1965. "America Takes the Lead" in John O'Brian, *Clement Greenberg: The Collected Essays and Criticism*. Chicago: University of Chicago Press.

    and

Sandler, Irving. 2009. *Abstract Expressionism and the American Experience : A Reevaluation*. Mission critical series. Lenox Mass.: Hard Press Editions.

2. Rosenberg, Harold. 1952. "The American Action Painters" in *The Tradition of the New*. London: Thames and Hudson.

3. Greenberg, Clement. 1955. "American-Type Painting" in *Art and Culture: Critical Essays*. Boston: Beacon Press.

4. Goosen, E.C.. "Rothko: The Omnibus Image" in *Art News*, January 1961.

New York abstract expressionists primarily lived, worked, painted and exhibited in a relatively small geographic area around 57th Street and, later, 10th Street. Artists and critics visited each other's studios, attended gallery openings and met weekly as groups to discuss contemporary art theory. Abstract Expressionism is often split chronologically into two segments: first and second-generation. The first-generation abstract expressionists matured during the WPA era and pioneered their new styles in the middle forties. This generation received the brunt of initial criticism and rejection and paved the way for acceptance of second-generation artists and the styles that followed the first-generation of abstract expressionists.[5] A wide range of artists who came to work in New York in the 1950s typifies the variety of the second-generation. They assembled themselves in schools and artists' co-ops along 10th Street and were all influenced by the work of the first-generation abstract expressionists who excited them with a newfound freedom of expression.[6]

Traditionally, Abstract Expressionism has been understood to include two modes or approaches, 'gestural' and 'color-field'. However, as implied by the variety of names by which the movement was originally known, the moniker Abstract Expressionism is hardly exact. The art was not always totally abstract nor expressionistic in the strictest sense of the words. While subject matters were generally abstracted to some degree, meaning that they were not 'true-to-life' depictions, many abstract expressionists, such as Willem de Kooning, still painted recognizable images. Expressionism held the implication that the work was painted to evoke emotions but the tone of those emotional responses varied widely. Situated within this nominal style were different methods of working that came to be called 'gestural' and 'color-field.' Gestural Abstract

---

5. Wood, Paul. 1993. *Modernism in Dispute: Art Since the Forties.* Modern art--practices and debates. New Haven: Yale University Press, in association with the Open University, London, 9-32.

　and

Polcari, Stephen. 1991. *Abstract Expressionism and the Modern Experience.* Cambridge England: Cambridge University Press, 4-16.

6. Sandler, Irving. 2009. *Abstract Expressionism and the American Experience : A Reevaluation.* Mission critical series. Lenox Mass.: Hard Press Editions.

　and

Sandler, Irving. 1978. *The New York School : The Painters and Sculptors of the Fifties.* Icon editions. New York: Harper & Row.

　and

Puniello, Françoise S., and Halina. Rusak. 1996. *Abstract Expressionist Women Painters: An Annotated Bibliography: Elaine De Kooning, Helen Frankenthaler, Grace Hartigan, Lee Krasner, Joan Mitchell, Ethel Schwabacher.* Lanham, Md.: Scarecrow Press, VII.

Expressionism includes art in which the process is evident in the final product, i.e. the gesture of the artist's application of paint is conjured in looking at the image—whether through paint pouring, as in the work of Jackson Pollock, or in heavy brushstrokes and impasto as in the work of Willem de Kooning. Abstract expressionists who worked in the color-field style often watered down their paints to create stains or washes that were then applied to the canvas without the obvious marking of the gestural approach to create color-studies or fields that became the sole subject matter. The art of Mark Rothko and Helen Frankenthaler are typical examples of color-field Abstract Expressionism. While gestural painting preceded color-field, both styles loosely embody the notion of abstraction and expressionism.[7]

Like most historical categorizations, our understanding of the movement now is shaped by stereotypes formed by generalizations used in vernacular language over time. In the case of Abstract Expressionism, this is largely due to the biases of popular art critics who shaped initial ideas about the style, principally Clement Greenberg. For Greenberg, abstract expressionist painting had to be large in scale, 'rough', emphasize the flatness of the canvas and, at least for 'gestural' painters, eschew color.[8] Greenberg and others advocated a 'lack of refinement' and exalted spontaneity and improvisation in the artistic process. The abstract-expressionist artist was characterized as rugged, masculine, embodying individualism.[9] However, these preconceptions constricted the definition of Abstract Expressionism

---

7. Sandler, Irving. 1970. *The Triumph of American Painting: A History of Abstract Expressionism*. New York: Praeger.
and

Sandler, Irving. 1978. *The New York School: The Painters and Sculptors of the Fifties*. Icon editions. New York: Harper & Row.
and

Sandler, Irving. 2009. *Abstract Expressionism and the American Experience: A Reevaluation*. Mission critical series. Lenox Mass.: Hard Press Editions.

8. See Greenberg, Clement. 1939. "Avant-Garde and Kitsch" in *Art and Culture: Critical Essays*. Boston: Beacon Press.
and

Greenberg, Clement. 1955. "American-Type Painting" in *Art and Culture: Critical Essays*. Boston: Beacon Press.
and

Greenberg, Clement. 1962. "After Abstract Expressionism" in John O'Brian. 1986. *The Collected Essays and Criticism*. Chicago: University of Chicago Press.

9. Greenberg, Clement. 1953. "Symposium: Is the French Avant-Garde Overrated?" in John O'Brian. 1986. *The Collected Essays and Criticism*. Chicago: University of Chicago Press.
and

Sandler, Irving. 2009. *Abstract Expressionism and the American Experience: A Reevaluation*. Mission critical series. Lenox Mass.: Hard Press Editions, 11-12.

and left many artists, such as Sally Hazelet Drummond, who did not agree with each of these tenets, out of consideration for inclusion in the conversation about what was the most progressive and advanced in contemporary art. Moreover, the connotation of the rugged individual artist working feverishly at the canvas created a strong sense of machismo in Abstract Expressionism. Artists, such as Drummond, who valued community and spirituality and whose work was deliberately created on an easel, or personal, scale rather than the 'herioic' size of paintings by artists such as Jackson Pollock or Clyfford Still — who were exploring an unrestrained use of color — contradicted traditional, Greenbergian, notions of Abstract Expressionism.

Alternatives To Conventional Abstract Expressionism

In contrast to Greenberg, critic and writer Irving Sandler advocated for a historical revision of the movement. Sandler was a contemporary of the second-generation abstract expressionists. He was the manager of the Tanager Gallery, the 10th Street artists' co-op that Sally Hazelet Drummond was a member of, from 1956 to 1959.[10] He is also one of the only major art critics to write about her art. In an exhibition Drummond had in 1984 at Artist Space, Sandler writes about the historical tendency to only remember conventional abstract expressionists, namely those whose work was 'gestural' and could even be described as violent, such as Willem de Kooning's *Women* Series. Expanding on this notion, Irving remarks: "In fact, fifties painting was far more varied than it is now remembered to have been. And if there was violence, there was also lyricism— and contemplation, none quieter than Drummond's abstract images." [11]

Sally Hazelet Drummond's Alternate Way

In this exhibition, looking at the work of Sally Hazelet Drummond, the viewer can begin to re-examine the conventional understanding of Abstract Expressionism and widen the sense of the movement and its impact. As Drummond's interview and her texts indicate, her path to abstraction was initially fairly conventional in that it began with a sense of liberation that the first-generation of abstract expressionist artists provided for the whole succeeding generation of followers. Like many of the leading abstract expressionists, the artist started painting figuratively. She describes her early taste in art as 'parochial'. Included in the exhibition is *Girl Sitting* from ca. 1940 which is an example of her early work. The work shows the influence of Cubism and perhaps some sense of earlier

---

10. Sandler, Irving. 2006. *From Avant-Garde to Pluralism: An On-The-Spot History*. Lenox, MA: Hard Press Editions, 33.

11. Sandler, Irving. 1984. "Sally Hazelet Drummond." Exhibition Handout, *Sally Hazelet Drummond: February 25-March 24*. Artists Space Gallery, New York.

20th century expressionism but is far from being abstract expressionistic. Recalling a 1947 visit to the Whitney Museum, the artist describes her early dislike of abstract art, "I can not help feeling that when the artist ceases to think even in terms of known recognizable objects that his finished canvases represent merely a conversation between himself…period."[12] Drummond goes on to state that for her in 1947, abstract — what she called non-objective art — was "terribly uninteresting."[13] Gradually, she started studying and being influenced by avant-garde artists such as Henri Matisse, Edvard Munch, Paul Klee and even Willem de Kooning.[14] *Girl in a Doorway*, 1949, and *Magician*, 1951 show the increasing influence of avant-gardism and initial contact with Abstract Expressionism in her art. In her 1952 master's thesis at the University of Louisville, Drummond outlines her changing perspective and preference for a more abstract expressionistic art. For Drummond, in 1947, the lack of recognizable subject matter was alienating to the viewer who had no commonality or entry-point into understanding the work but it is apparent that her opinion had changed by the early 1950s. By then, she seems to be in agreement with the first-generation of abstract expressionists, who saw the elimination of the subject matter as a means of elevating art. Without a subject to distract the viewer, the focus became solely on the formal elements of the art and the raw expression of the individual artist — lines, shapes, colors and textures were universal archetypes and metaphors that were a democratizing measure for viewers in which little to no preconceived understanding was requisite (i.e. the viewer did not have to know the story of Sophocles' Antigone in order to understand the art—the feeling or emotion, 'expression', was conveyed through the abstract formal elements of the work). Her 1952 thesis goes on to trace her journey into abstraction; Drummond recounts a time in which after painting a vase of flowers she began to add white paint until the entire canvas was covered with the exception of small areas and the original image was no longer visible. Drummond had veered into Abstract Expressionism.[15] Upon the completion of her master's degree in painting, Drummond's work had become abstract expressionistic in the traditional sense, as can be seen in works such as *Untitled*, ca. 1952. There is no recognizable subject matter, there is little color in the work and the presence of the gesture is evident.

---

12. Hazelet, Sally. 1952. "A Commentary on my Painting." Master's thesis, University of Louisville, 6.

13. Ibid.

14. Drummond, Sally Hazelet. 1989. "Gallery Talk for Rollins College." Artist's papers.

15. Hazelet, Sally. 1952. "A Commentary on my Painting." Master's thesis, University of Louisville, 17.

When Drummond joined the Tanager Gallery in New York in 1953, her work was similar to *Untitled*. The artist describes her artistic process and intent in her 1952 text on page 33. Under the influence of the 10th Street scene, Drummond's work continued to evolve into monochromatic studies with only a hint of an image in the center of the canvas. Drummond describes these works in the text titled the "World of Silent Painting" (see page 34 in this catalogue): "My present paintings each have a single color uninterrupted by line or shape. The color is laid on in a series of thin glazes restricted to subtle variations within the narrow limits of the dominating color. In the center of each painting is a concentration or deepening of tone, which serves as a focus or core of the painting."[16] For Drummond, the departure from the 'gestural' style to the 'color-field' style was a means of leaving behind much of the individualism and chance for what she calls a 'World of Silent Painting,' the quieter and lyrical Abstract Expressionism Sandler wrote about in 1984.

While none of these early monochromatic canvases exist, a slide of work in this vein has been reproduced on page 29. The relationship of this work to her mature style is evident in the use of all over patterning and the central core imagery. As Drummond outlined in her gallery talk at Rollins College in 1989 she discovered pointillism in 1958 after seeing a retrospective of pointillist Georges Seurat at the Museum of Modern Art. Inspired by his use of dots "in giving a sense of volume and energy to simple shapes."[17] Drummond goes on to explain that this was the mechanism she had been looking for to activate her earlier canvases and that she started experimenting with the method in *Bluebird*, 1960, and *Heart of Iron*, ca. 1960. These works show some early results of the artist's application of pointillism. These dots are larger and further apart than in later works indicating that she continued to refine her pointillist technique for the rest of her career.

The last major change to take place in Drummond's art is the changing of the center core from dark to light. Also outlined in her 1989 gallery talk (see page 38) the artist muses, "In the 1960's my paintings had a dark center. I think I felt that the core should have weight, that the center needed to be anchored down." However, after the suggestion of Lois Dodd, a fellow Tanager Gallery member, Drummond began experimenting with a light center. In her words, "it gradually

---

16. Hazelet, Sally. "World of Silent Painting." In *Arts in Louisville Magazine*, September, 1957.

17. Drummond, Sally Hazelet. 1989. "Gallery Talk for Rollins College." Artist's papers.

became, not a matter of anchoring but of searching for a kind of radiance."[18] All of the exhibited works from *A Simple Arrangement*, 1969, to *Untitled (Gold Leaf)*, 2010 have light centers. While Drummond experienced major changes in her pictorial style early on in her journey to abstraction, the artist describes her venture from her early abstractions to color-field painting to the contemplative and quiet radiant style that she discovered in the early 1960's: in this "narrow path"[19] she established her personal working identity and a consistent oeuvre.

Drummond's Iconoclasm

A deeper look at a single work of Drummond's oeuvre is revealing. In *No Separation* from 1991, many of the affinities and departures from traditional Abstract Expressionism become apparent. Her independence and determination to follow her own course become apparent when approaching the canvas from a distance: the scale is unassertive at 36"x36" compared to the 'heroic' scale of many abstract expressionist works. At first, the painting appears to be an off-white color with some variations of color. Upon closer examination, a myriad of colors become apparent — the blues, purples, pinks, yellows, greens in several hues placed one right next to another are not the subdued palette of conventional 'gestural' painters. Even while this bold use of color nods to the work of 'color-field' painters who were emboldened by strong hues, the scale and variety of colors applied without washes in petite dots is unique to Drummond's work. Ultimately however, the dots themselves are an affirmation of the ideology of the gesture of abstract expressionists but their deliberate application contradicts what the artist called "the bacchanalian orgy of paint throwing, dripping and splashing"[20] in her 1989 gallery talk. When studying *No Separation* it becomes apparent that the profusion of the carefully placed and carefully chosen colors of her dots as they trace and build the image dot by dot, as well as the overall nature of her composition, guides the viewer to a metaphorical understanding of the artist's view of the seemingly limitless connections within the piece—and life. The canvas was painted methodically, again challenging the conventional notions of the feverish abstract expressionist. This approach also requires more from the viewer; as opposed to the brashness of many conventional abstract expressionist works, Drummond's art necessitates a more contemplative approach. *No Separation*, while one work out of many, typifies how Sally Hazelet Drummond disputes and expands the territory of Abstract Expressionism.

---

18. Ibid.

19. Ibid.

20. Ibid.

Abstract Expressionism embodied an iconoclastic spirit and pushed the boundaries of artistic freedom. It was this impetus that propelled many second-generation abstract expressionists, including Sally Hazelet Drummond. However, the historical tendency to categorize and generalize the movement has ultimately led to a narrower conception of Abstract Expressionism than what actually transpired in artists' studios. For an art that was intended to simplify and universalize the art experience for the individual, to be all about primal connections, as Drummond stated in her 1989 gallery talk, her work refutes the notion of the lone artistic genius and rugged individualist and serves instead as a visual paradigm of carefully considered and placed individual dots building an overall composition that echoes and reflects the artistic 10th Street community in which she lived, worked and developed her signature style.[21] Her 'quieter' abstraction achieved the artist's goals of creating a contemplative environment for the viewer. While Drummond has been described as anticipating several succeeding genres such as Minimalism and Op-Art, she is, in fact, a Second-Generation Abstract Expressionist—a continuing, determined, subversive freethinker. Drummond once described Abstract Expressionism as having a type of "iconoclastic fervor"[22] in its desire to actively challenge and create a new art form from its predecessors but her own ability to challenge the popular conventions of the movement through her long career of artmaking is in itself a tremendous example of iconoclastic fervor.

---

21. Ibid.

22. Hazelet, Sally. 1952. "A Commentary on my Painting." Master's thesis, University of Louisville, 14.

A Conversation with Lois Dodd about Sally Hazelet Drummond

Lois Dodd was one of the founding members of the Tanager Gallery and was the only other woman in the gallery. Drummond and Dodd have remained close friends. Dodd's insights on her friend illuminate the artist's early work, associations, and career.

Dodd's reluctance to label Drummond's work as abstract expressionist reveals the strong connotation implied by the term Abstract Expressionism and the need to revisit the movement in order to rediscover and highlight the myriad ways abstraction and expressionism were explored by these artists.

Cajori, one of the five founding members of the Tanager Gallery in 1952, had met Sally while both studied with John Heliker at Columbia University. He brought her to meet with us. We liked Sally and her work and invited her to become a member of the gallery.

Sally lived in the block of E. 10th Street just east of the gallery and I often stopped by with my young son to visit Sally and Cleo, her French poodle. She sometimes babysat for me and we sometimes kept Cleo if Sally had to be away for a time.

I remember those early paintings being monochromatic, not too brushy, and shiny. Her pointillist technique came somewhat later. The artist in the gallery whose work was closet to Sally's was Ben Isquith. Ben was working monochromatically also, but

left painting for involvement in cybernetics and then died at a rather young age. Sally was friends with Lutz Sander whose work has some relationship to hers. Lutz was a member of the abstract expressionist generation whose work was abstract but not expressionistic.

The artists of the Tanager Gallery were quite divergent in their approaches to painting. Sally's work was admired and appreciated but not imitated by any other member.

For me, Sally's work is most closely related to Richard Pousette-Dart as far as technique and form go. Her spirituality and mood closely relate to Rothko but I have no idea if either of them had that intent. Certainly during the 50's and 60's there were many artists interested in Zen Buddhism and many of us read *Zen in the Art of Archery*.

I own a painting of Sally's from 1973.
On the back is a taped a statement
as follows:

> *Form is no other than
> emptiness, emptiness no other
> than form.*
>
> *Form is precisely emptiness,
> emptiness precisely form.*
>
> *- From the Heart Sutra*

I question the use of the term Abstract
Expressionism to describe Sally's work
of the 1950's and beyond. Abstract, yes.
Expressionism, no.

Our generation, younger than the abstract
expressionist by 10, 15 and 20 years revered
and admired what they were doing. De
Kooning, Kline and Guston with studios
nearby came into the Tanager Gallery. They
encouraged and supported our efforts. Jack
Tworkov contributed some money on one
occasion.

As artist's lives go, Sally's has been quite
successful. Her work was picked up by
Richard Bellamy and shown uptown at his
gallery, the Green Gallery. Richard knew her
work from the 10th Street days as he was
involved with one of the Co-Ops earlier. I
believe this happened before the close of
the Tanager in 1962 or there abouts. So,
Sally's work has steadily been represented
by some gallery. After Fischbach there was
a period of time before Alexandre Gallery
picked up her work. All of these galleries
are reputable but she did suffer from her
lack of sales. It clearly depends on what one
considers success to be. But I know Sally to
be a developed, strong artist.

Lois Dodd

An Interview with the Artist

Germantown, New York, July 25th, 2015

*The following is an abridged account of an interview with the artist Sally Hazelet Drummond (**SHD**) by the curator, Hillary Sullivan (**HS**) on July 25th, 2015 at her residence in Germantown, New York.*

HS: Sally Hazelet Drummond, considering the show is a celebration of your career and ties into your alma mater and relationship with Louisville, lets talk about your graduate school days in the 1950s. How did you get to Louisville?

SHD: My parents where living there. They moved there around 1951 I would say. I was getting a master's in painting. I took the required work for a master's and I went there because my parents were there.

HS: Did you like the program or was it just a matter of necessity of what was near?

SHD: It was more of necessity.

HS: What were some of your influences in Louisville?

SHD: Mostly, I think the main influence were my teachers. When I had an interesting teacher, I was more interested. I loved Ulfert Wilke's work

HS: You studied under Ulfert Wilke at the University of Louisville.

SHD: Well you see, I liked him so I liked his teaching. He was very much an artist. He was a good painter. He was very enthusiastic and was high energy. He was German and talked really fast as I remember.

HS: It was during this time that you started to move into abstraction—did he let you experiment and encourage this change?

SHD: Pretty much.

HS: And where did you paint when you were in Louisville? At your parents' house?

SHD: They had a house. A nice house called Microphylla by the previous owners. There was a studio there. It was charming because it had a fireplace.

HS: Did people like your art in Louisville?

SHD: Not particularly.

HS: Why do you think not?

SHD: Well I didn't know many people in Louisville and I didn't know hardly any artists, I might have known one or two. But it was not an art environment. Louisville is quite conservative.

HS: Okay. Now, we're going to have a show in Louisville again and you haven't had one there since 1990 — what do you want the show to demonstrate to the city and to the state that it didn't understand before?
SHD: Nothing. That's up to them.

HS: Do you think reactions will be different?
SHD: Well they might be. They've lived different lives and I've lived different lives.

HS: What do you expect from your audience when they go and they look at one of your paintings?
SHD: I don't expect anything from them but I'm thrilled when they like it.

HS: After Louisville, you went to Italy on a Fulbright Scholarship.
SHD: Oh yes. That was wonderful. Just to be there, to see the wonderful works of art. It's just fabulous.

HS: And then you moved to New York?
SHD: I wanted to come to New York because that's where the action was. I lived on Tenth Street. I joined a gallery. It was a co-operative gallery.

HS: The Tanager, an artists-run gallery, a rather unconventional model at the time.
SHD: I guess so.

HS: What was it like being in that environment?
SHD: In New York there was such an atmosphere. Friends and the atmosphere in New York was so different. It was sympathetic. I adored the arts. I love New York. I still love New York. I do. I think it's wonderful. I feel alive there. And being in New York was a great stimulus. It is a wonderful place. I liked it a lot. I loved being in New York knowing artists but I love being in New York period.

HS: And what about in the Tanager and the Tenth Street Galleries?
SHD: Oh, and Tenth Street was very nice.

Laughter

HS: What was nice?
SHD: The artists. Serious artists lived and worked there on Tenth Street.

HS: Who were some of the most influential artists for you at the time?
SHD: Oh, De Kooning. De Kooning. De Kooning. De Kooning.

HS: Which De Kooning?
SHD: The man and the woman? Oh, the man, Mr. De Kooning. I liked De Kooning's work. I still like it.

HS: He was certainly better known at the time.
SHD: He' s a better painter too.

HS: You met him, you knew him?
SHD: Well I met him. I also knew
lousy artists.

HS: They were lousy because…
SHD: Never any talent and when I was
living in New York, I went to quite a few
artists' shows and Tenth Street was also
lively in those days.

HS: I can imagine. That environment was
really a crucible for American Abstract
Expressionism.
SHD: It had good openings.

HS: Well attended?
SHD: And cheap wine.

Laughter

HS: Now this was one of the first times that
you were able to make art unencumbered
by the oversight of academia and you were
in the stimulating environment of Tenth
Street—did you experiment with your art
making during this time?
SHD: I guess I could experiment.

HS: Did you?
SHD: No.

HS: No?
SHD: No.

Laughter

HS: Why not?
SHD: I'm not an experimenter.

HS: You said that you're not an
experimenter; you don't like to change
much. But you've had a couple of major
changes in your career. For one, in the very
beginning, you were painting figuratively.
SHD: Yes.

HS: Subjects that looked exactly like what
they were supposed to be, that you could
tell what it was. And then you started
working in more abstract, cerebral terms.
What do you think motivated that change?
SHD: Well I think it was seeing work that
I thought was good. I always wanted to
be good.

HS: Always wanted to be good. For whom?
SHD: Myself. I'm always seeking, I've
always sought to be good. Of course,
I wanted to be good and I liked good
painting. But that was about all I could say
on that subject.

HS: Did the other artists think that you
were good?
SHD: They ignored me. Often I was pretty
much ignored.

HS: By male artists, critics and curators?
SHD: And female.

HS: Did that bother you?
SHD: Well prejudice in any form
bothers me.

HS: What was is like being a female artist in that scene in the early 50s-60s?
SHD: I never thought about it.

HS: You never thought of it?
SHD: I was interested in painting and the fact that I was a woman never occurred to me. Never did.

HS: Surely it occurred to others at that time.
SHD: I acknowledge that it was difficult being a woman and being a painter. It's true, there is a prejudice against women.

HS: Do you personally remember any biases? You were in an environment where there were very few women at the time—especially in Abstract Expressionism.
SHD: Yes, I think it was there. But I never thought about it much.

HS: Towards the end of the Tanager Gallery you got married to Wick Drummond from Louisville, Kentucky and had your son, Craig Drummond. What was it like caring for a baby while trying to break into the professional art scene?
SHD: Oh. Well it wasn't easy but it worked. Having a baby is difficult. I felt responsible for his, for his bringing up. I looked after Wick too.

HS: The Tanager Gallery closed shortly after Craig was born in 1962 and you moved out of the city. First to Connecticut and later to Germantown, New York where you live now.
SHD: Yes.

HS: Then you received a Guggenheim Fellowship and opted to move to France for a year. How was that experience?
SHD: It wasn't easy, we had to find a place to live and paint and raise a family. I had a small studio. I painted.

HS: By the late 1950s and early 1960s you were painting the starburst-like images for which you are now known, can you talk about your process?
SHD: Well I cover with a base color all over and I put a little in the middle. One painting leads to another painting.

HS: You started in the middle.
SHD: The middle and work out.

HS: To the edge? Now how do you pick what color each of the dots is going to be?
SHD: One color leads to another.

HS: So you start with one color and then you start adding colors on top?
SHD: Yes.

HS: How would you pick which color to use?
SHD: The painting that went before usually dictates what comes afterwards.

HS: So you put the dots on—how do you apply the dots?
SHD: With a little brush. *Laughs*

HS: Now your dots—it seems that they get smaller. In the earlier paintings, the dots are bigger and in the later paintings they're smaller and farther apart.
SHD: Well I think that's because I wanted an intensity.

HS: You wanted an intensity. With the smaller dots?
SHD: *Nods*

HS: You've written elsewhere that you started using dots after seeing a retrospective of Georges Seurat in 1958 at the Museum of Modern Art. What attracted you to the use of dots?
SHD: Well, Seurat's had an energy to them.

HS: Do your dots have an energy?
SHD: I think the use of dots does.

HS: Your earlier works had a darker center and then you moved to painting light centers.
SHD: Yes, its about separation because… actually, Lois Dodd suggested I make them light in the center.

HS: Lois Dodd, the only other woman in the Tanager Gallery, told you to make them light in the center?
SHD: Yes. I did and I liked what I saw. They're light around the edges and I like that. They seem to have a certain spirit.

HS: Is that spirit different than when the center is dark?
SHD: Yes, because with light in the center, there's a certain exuberance that they didn't have before.

HS: What kind of mood would you be in when you would sit down to paint?
SHD: It's just something I did. It wasn't a matter of taste. I just, I just, wanted to do it. And I was interested in it.

HS: Was it a chore?
SHD: No, no.

HS: But it something that you felt you had to do?
SHD: Yes. I had to do it. Well, I think it was a just and noble pursuit and there was a lot that I disapproved of. Lots, lots that I didn't really enjoy.

HS: In the art being made at the time?
SHD: Yes.

HS: So you made something that you enjoyed.
SHD: Yes. There wasn't any mission.

HS: What was different about the work that you were producing?
SHD: I was trying, I wasn't sure of anything then. I wasn't sure. I think I was always doubtful.

HS: About the art around you?
SHD: And my own work too.

HS: Is your art personal? When you paint is it about you?
SHD: No.

HS: Do you put yourself in it?
SHD: Well it's I that painted it—that says its mine. It's about me. It's personal in the sense that I made it.

HS: Can people, when they look at it, can they tell anything about you?
SHD: No. Well, I guess they could. But not anything very interesting.

Laughter

HS: How do you describe your work?
SHD: Well, I'd say its contemplative.

HS: Contemplative.
SHD: Describes it pretty well.

HS: What do you expect people to contemplate when they look at it?
SHD: It has to mean something to them.

HS: Many viewers have described your work as spiritual, now would say that your art is spiritual?
SHD: Well I don't see it as spiritual. It may have a spiritual quality to it. It doesn't seem to make sense but I think that it has a spiritual quality to it.

HS: What do you expect from your viewers when they look at your work?
SHD: I don't expect anything from them but I'm thrilled when they like it.

HS: You're thrilled when they like it. Why is that?
SHD: Oh, I think you always want to be liked.

Laughter

HS: Speaking of being liked, you have a line in your thesis that discusses the over-abundance of art critics. At one point you jest that there are more art critics than actual artists.

Laughter

HS: Basically lambasting art criticism. What is the role of art critics today? Or what is the role of art criticism in general?
SHD: I don't think there is a big role. People are going to like your work or not like your work. It makes no difference in the matter of what style it is.

HS: Is the amount or degree to which people like your art a measure of success for an artist?

SHD: A successful artist is an artist who sells his work. That makes success.

HS: That makes success?

SHD: Yes, I think so.

HS: Would you say you're successful? I would say you're successful.

SHD: Well, compared to whom? Compared to a lot of artists, I'm not successful. To some artists, a number, I am.

HS: I think for me, and where I'm getting at is that you talk about how you made artwork for yourself. I asked, 'when did you know it was good?' and you answered that you knew it was good when you liked it.

SHD: *Laughs.* Okay.

HS: Most of your career, you've created for yourself more than you've made art for other people.

SHD: Yes.

HS: And the fact that you were able to stay true and to do what you wanted when everybody around you had an opinion…

SHD: Yes.

HS: I think that's a mark of success.

SHD: *Laughs.* Okay.

HS: What are your thoughts?

SHD: Well, that's not how I would define success. No, successful is sold.

HS: So the art market is what determines success for the arts?

SHD: Yes.

HS: Okay. Now what has been your relationship and role with the art market?

SHD: *Laughs. Makes surprised face.*

Laughter

HS: So you weren't trying to successful?

SHD: No. A., I wanted to paint and B., It was that kind of work. You are always influenced by somebody or something. At least that's been my experience. Everybody, every person, every family has a history. People should know that I had a lot of enthusiasms.

Sally Hazelet Drummond's interview is telling in many respects. With both brevity and honesty, she talked about her career as an artist, her view on the art establishment and, most fervently, her love of New York City. Taken over the course of several sessions throughout the day on the back porch of her Germantown residence, it felt like visiting a friend.

Admittedly, I started with her time in Louisville due to my own biases but her graduate school days also mark her continued exploration into Abstract Expressionism. The thesis that she wrote upon graduation focuses almost exclusively on her transition from figurative work to abstraction. Additionally, Ulfert Wilke, her professor at the University of Louisville, was an abstract expressionist with strong West Coast influences. Tracking her career path after graduation is also informative in her journey to abstraction based on her influences and interactions at the time. As mentioned in the interview, the Tanager Gallery was a crystalizing moment for the artist. The gallery, the most famous of the Tenth Street artist co-ops, was the epicenter of Abstract Expressionism. Undoubtedly, the Tanager and the Tenth Street Gallery scene was the greatest contributing factor in Drummond's work and the expanded notion of Abstract Expressionism as proposed by the curator. Tellingly, the artist's desire to make 'good' art and the pressure of the art market are highly symptomatic of abstract expressionist art criticism, especially that written by Clement Greenburg, demonstrating the artist's affinity with the movement. Drummond's description of her artistic process also reveals her footing in Abstract Expressionism in her use of gesture, through dots, and the symbiotic relationship of colors seemingly unconsciously applied. However, the artist's version of Abstract Expressionism deviates from the conventional model in its spiritual quality and sense of community as outlined in the interview.

The full interview can be found in the addendum for Hillary Sullivan's 2015 thesis at the University of Louisville.

Blue Painting
1957
Oil on Canvas
40"x46"
Present Location Unknown

Selected
Artist's
Statements

The statements included in this section were all written by Sally Hazelet Drummond between 1952 and 1989 and were collected from the artist's papers. The curator, Hillary Sullivan, selected these statements and speeches to elucidate the artist's career, her journey into abstraction and the iconoclastic spirit embodied both in Abstract Expressionism and in her own approach to the style.

As argued in the catalogue essay, the exhibition, through the work of Sally Hazelet Drummond, advocates for and presents an expanded view of Abstract Expressionism. As demonstrated by the artist's work, Abstract Expressionism was not always a product of happenstantial gesture and machismo posturing but was often intentionally subtle, carefully considered and just as inherently spiritual and emotive.

Previous page: Detail of *Heart of Iron*, c. 1960, Oil on Canvas, 60" x 60", ©Sally Hazelet Drummond, courtesy Alexandre Gallery, New York

Simple Abstraction
1952

Written the year of Sally Hazelet Drummond's graduation from the University of Louisville with a master's in painting in 1952, this text demonstrates her grounding in traditional abstract expressionist tenets – chiefly, the emphasis on chance and her semi-automatic art making process. While Drummond continued to work in a semi-automatic manner typical of conventional Abstract Expressionism, the shift in her work in the mid-to-late 1950s is what is considered in this exhibition to expand the understanding of Abstract Expressionism.

In my recent paintings I have tried to express forms emerging in space, forms that have no particular beginning or ending but which are in a state of flux and change. Most of the forms appear as accidental occurrences. I do not consider these as mere designs but as statements that derive their authority from nature. Chance and accident are constantly at work in nature. They can result in great beauty. I try to recognize and to preserve those images that are meaningful and to reject those that are not.

I never make preparatory sketches, preferring to work from a semi-automatic beginning, directly on the board, building up the surface of the painting, and finally, to allow a few images to make their appearance. By reducing the number of forms to a minimum, I hope to gain a simplicity and directness of expression.

A single tree on the horizon expresses as majestically as a forest does the nature and function of a tree. A piano sonata can be as moving an experience as a symphony for full orchestra. My particular preference is for the simple rather than for the complex expressions. Both types of approach are valid.

World of Silent Painting

Arts in Louisville Magazine, September 1957

*The following is an excerpt from an artist statement Sally Hazelet Drummond wrote for **Arts in Louisville Magazine** in September of 1957, only a year before she pioneered her trademark pointillist style. Drummond describes her early 1950s work, pieces such as **Untitled**, as being typically abstract expressionist in its use of gestural swabs and abstracted subject matter. The artist then discusses the shift in her art making that led to a simpler painting method of largely monochromatic canvases with colored washes drawn into a darker center.*

While no canvases from this stage exists, the correlation to her later work can clearly be seen in the use of dominant coloring with subtle variations and the use of a compositional method that utilizes central core patterning. A slide of this work has been reproduced on page 29.

Drummond's description of Abstract Expressionism is telling in that it relies heavily on assumptions about the movement as defined by the critic Clement Greenberg. Also revealing is the artist's own independent expansion of her understanding of the movement by the self-labeling of her work as 'Silent Painting,' a term that implied that there were subtler aspects of Abstract Expressionism to be explored that would promote an expanded view of the movement which the curator of this exhibition seeks to advance.

Those things which an artist reads, feels, observes, and inherits from the past constitutes his character and viewpoint; after a while these influences begin to form a pattern and direction. My direction has been from the complex toward the simple.

My present style of painting grew out of earlier abstract expressionistic paintings. Abstract Expressionism has many adherents among contemporary painters. A kind of iconoclastic fervor describes these paintings. Interweaving, pulsing, kinetic lines, shapes and color intuitively released during the process of painting are the principal aesthetic agents. The introduction of a figure or landscape is used as something to pull apart and fragmentize. Abstract Expressionism is an assertion in exaggerated and powerful terms of a world personally created by the artist and a denial that the function of the artist is to record and catalogue events in nature as seen by the physical eye.

My paintings were influenced by some of these abstract expressionistic canvases which pushed freedom to the nth degree. The paint was applied in heavy strokes, thin strokes; it was alternatively dripped or daubed on the canvas depending on the intuitive impulse. I strove for movement, and exhilaration. Forms were sought that were open, spontaneous and full of suspense. However, one tendency began to emerge and later to persist which was ultimately to lead to my present paintings. Although I usually began a painting with a heavy undergrowth of shapes and colors the final form of the painting evolved after a reduction and simplification of the original statement. Sometimes this process of eliminating lines and shapes would continue to the point where only small islands of the earlier complexity remained. Perhaps this superficial desire for fewer forms grew out of a subconscious search for a purer, more impersonal expression. I don't know. I do know that gradually bit by bit I left the exuberant cacophonic world of Abstract Expressionism and entered a world of "silent painting."

My present paintings each have a single color uninterrupted by line or shape. The color is laid on in a series of thin glazes restricted to subtle variations within the narrow limits of the dominating color. In the center of each painting is a concentration or deepening of tone, which serves as a focus or core of the painting.

 For me, color is the basic ingredient of painting, and it is with color that I try to express my feelings. The outer form of my paintings is the shape of the canvas. The inner form is striven for through the depth and richness of the color. Cezanne said, "When the color is at its richest, the form is at its plenitude." My ultimate goal is to create a single radiant field of

contemplation where form and content have become one. In 1908 Matisse said, "What I dream of is an art equilibrated, pure and calm, free of disturbing subject-matter, an art that for any intellectual worker, or business man or writer can be a means of soothing the soul, something like a comfortable armchair in which one can recover from physical fatigue."

I am trying to affirm something that I believe—that underneath all the complexities and contradictions in nature there is a silent, pure, and eternal presence and force. I feel that love is expressed strongest in terms of quietude and simplicity—that 'less is more.' In some things it is a fine line that separates something from nothing. In my work there is the constant danger of falling into meaningless emptiness. But this very danger constitutes the challenge.

I do not respond to subject-matter in paintings, as the term is generally understood, except on a superficial level. Those feelings of identification or nostalgia evoked by subject-matter, I believe, are not the essential qualities which define the value of a work of art. If they were, any religious picture would be better than any still life. As in all things, it is a matter of the spirit. It is the nameless essence which lies underneath the subject-matter that I am concerned with. The deep truth is imageless.

-Reprinted from **Arts in Louisville Magazine**, *September 1957*

Great Art
Undated

While the exact date of this text is unknown, it appears to have been written around 1965. This idealistic text reveals much of Sally Hazelet Drummond's belief that art is transcendent. Moreover, the artist again references the influences of impressionism and pointillism but also Abstract Expressionism. Tellingly, the sources she cites here, Philip Guston and Ad Reinhardt were also quieter examples of Abstract Expressionism. Like Drummond, these artists also fit into the expanded definition of Abstract Expressionism explored by this exhibition in their tendency to strive for refinement and simplicity. Lastly, Drummond mentions the viewer's participation in the artistic process and her belief in community and interdependence through her wish that viewers feel the restorative powers of her art.

I believe that all great art is an attempt on the part of the artist to express his faith in the unseen, but intuitively felt structured and infinite beauty lying inherent in the visible world. This faith and concern, I believe, is what binds together all the highest forms of artistic expressions of man down through the ages.

I believe there exists within the complex of nature, one pure undifferentiated power. It is eternal and creates expanding form out of inert matter, gives direction to undisciplined energy.

My vision is of an art that declares this sensed reality in the purest and simplest terms — the total painting as the image — silent, emphatic and radiant.

Nothing exists in a vacuum. All art worthy of the name grows out of a tradition and into something that is of its' own time. The roots of my work, I believe, are to be found in the concern with atmospheric light of the French Impressionists and the pointillism of the Post-Impressionist painter Georges Seurat. In my own time, the non-objective experiments of Abstract Expressionism of the mid 1950's as represented by the work of Philip Guston and the austerity and minimalism seen in the paintings of Ad Reinhardt of the 1960's drew me into what has been a central concern for almost 30 years. For me, the challenge and significance of 20th Century art from the time of Cezanne has been the attempt to simplify and to reduce the complexities of the visual world to essential and meaningful forms. This search for essences has been a thread which to me distinguishes art of this century from most Western art since the Italian Renaissance.

This is a process of distilling one's perceptions, of shedding extraneous concerns. The challenge of this quest is to present a form that will be emotionally fulfilling and pulsating with life and energy. I would hope that the viewer of my paintings would feel warmed, refreshed and at peace.

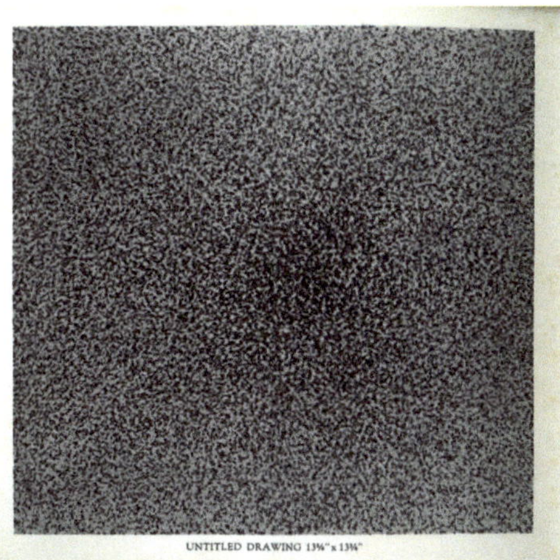

Exhibition Brochure
Sally Hazelet
Solo Exhibition
Tanager Gallery
April 1 - April 21, 1960
90 E 10th Street, New York, New York

———————————————

Artist's Papers

Gallery Talk

Cornell Art Gallery, Rollins College, September 25, 1989

The following is an excerpt from a speech Sally Hazelet Drummond gave at Cornell Art Gallery at Rollins College in Winter Park, Florida September 25, 1989.

The text is largely autobiographical but provides crucial insights into Drummond's career, influences and journey to abstraction. In simple and honest statements the artist reveals her values of interconnectivity, simple beauty and emotional complexities that were often at odds with the virile environment of conventional Abstract Expressionism in the 1950s.

Like many other statements by the artist, her reaction against much of the 'ego-dripping' of the time and her own artistic response questioned the conventional understanding of the movement. Through her work, Abstract Expressionism can also be seen to include purposeful direction, inclusion and interdependence and transcendence.

I like to think of my work as having something to do with connections. I like the concept of connections. When connections are made between things, individuals, families, communities, nations, planets — it makes me feel good.

I also like color and light. So you could say my paintings are about light, color and connections — no separations, no up no down, no left no right, no shape no forms, the whole painting as the image.

Life is so complex maybe that is one reason I have been attempting to simplify, simplify. Since the middle of the 1950's I have followed this narrow path pretty relentlessly. However, it took me a while before I found within myself who I was as an artist or rather where I wanted to be. Maybe it was just a matter of becoming less influenced by other artists and more by own efforts. And so I thought I would describe to you a little how I arrived at my current paintings.

In 1942 while a freshman at Rollins I took a sculpture course given by Constance Ortmayer. She was a wonderful teacher and an accomplished sculptor. Miss Ortmayer was the kind of teacher who, after a few weeks of instruction would let you work alone and just as you were about to explode with frustration because maybe the eyes that weren't right or the mouth was really weird, quietly at your elbow she would appear and Mother Theresa-like with just the lightest pressure of the thumbs would make it work. I am sorry I never saw Miss Ortmayer after 1944 as that was my last year here. I transferred from Rollins after my sophomore year. The idea of living in New York City had taken hold of me.

My parents looked upon my desire to live in New York with a collective dim eye and prevailed upon me to postpone moving there for a year and suggested I stop for a year in Washington, D.C. where my sister lived with her husband who was stationed in Fort Belvoir, Virginia. This was 1944 and World War II was still raging. I lived at the King-Smith School in Washington where I took some classes, one in sculpture, and worked part-time in a bookstore.

In 1945 I moved to New York and enrolled in the school of General Studies at Columbia University from which I received my bachelor's degree in 1948. At Columbia I debated whether to major in philosophy or art and ultimately chose painting. I had hoped to take sculpture and painting but at that school the two programs were separate and distinct. I think living in New York was as much of an influence on my development as a painter as my university study. I saw a lot of theatre, modern dance — Martha Graham, Merce Cunningham, Jose Limon — and went to a lot of foreign films. Of course, the opportunity to see the great original collections of the Metropolitan, Whitney, Brooklyn, Museum of Modern Art and the galleries along 57th Street was also of enormous value.

The painter, John Heliker, was teaching at Columbia while I was there. In fact, he had a long and distinguished career there in addition to his success as a professional painter. I've had quite a few art teachers since I have bounced around a bit from school to school and frequently encountered artists with surprisingly closed minds. Most of these artists had a narrow agenda that they attempted to foist onto their students but John Heliker was not one of these. He used to say that he was pleased if some of his students were not aware of his style of painting. He genuinely encouraged us to find our own path.

My tastes in art were pretty parochial and conservative when I arrived at Columbia and John opened up all kinds of doors to his students. He didn't try to push us through those doors, he just opened the doors and he had a vital interest in all the arts. Among his friends were John Cage and Merce Cunningham. He spoke of the poetry of Rainer Maria Rilke, Gerard Manley Hopkins and the painting of Paul Klee. He moved in a corner of the avant-garde that was totally foreign to me – puzzling and intriguing at the same time.

Also at Columbia there was a student teacher, Eleanor Heuser, who introduced me to the work of Edvard Munch the Norwegian painter who lived during the early part of this century. His world was an enormous psychodrama of rage, jealousy and guilt simply and powerfully presented – very emotional and direct. I loved them.

Just about the time I discovered Edvard Munch I attended the premier of Gian-Carlo Menotti's opera "The Medium." Perhaps some of you have seen it and are familiar with the story. Its not a long opera and has only about five characters. It's a gloomy piece involving a charlatan who preys upon those who have lost a loved one by claiming to be able to communicate with the dead. Her wraith-like daughter was her mother's accomplice by appearing as the returned spirit of the deceased.

I don't remember whether I was bowled over by this opera but I do remember that it gave me an idea for a painting which I began the next day in school and out of which grew two or three related paintings combining the influence of Edvard Munch and Menotti's opera. They were paintings of slightly distorted interiors with one or two slightly haunted figures. Pretty gloomy and moody. I mention these paintings not because they were especially good, they weren't, but because for the first time in my life after three or four years of drifting around stylistically, I felt that whatever they were, they were mine.

After graduating from Columbia, I attended the Institute of Design in Chicago, a modern school of design founded by Moholy-Nagy. I remained there for one and a half years taking their foundation course, courses in two and three dimensional design—quite a shift away from the world of Edvard Munch. I lived first in a rooming house and later in a basement apartment and continued to paint independently of my design work at the institute. My painting at this time flip-flopped around from the influence to influence, from Paul Klee to Robert Motherwell to Picasso, and also showed influences of two excellent teachers there — Hugo Weber and Emerson Woelffer.

After the Institute of Design, I enrolled in the University of Louisville where my family now lived. I studied and painted there for two years in order to receive a master's degree in painting. Edward Melcarth and Ulfert Wilke were my principal teachers. Ulfert talked a great deal about contemporary American artists working mostly in New York and he spoke a lot about Willem De Kooning.

De Kooning was an enormous influence on a lot of young artists and was the driving force of Abstract Expressionism. I too was caught up in the energy, freedom, directness, strength and physicality of his paintings. I wonder if Rock and Roll functions today in our culture somewhat like Abstract Expressionism functioned in the 1950's. There was such a sweep to his canvases and the energy didn't stop at the edges, it was propelled beyond them. It was kind of a magnificent informed chaos that De Kooning presented.

In 1952 I spent the year in Venice, Italy. At this time I painted with lacquer paint because it dried fast. Ulfert Wilke had introduced me to this medium. After I returned from a year abroad someone asked me to what extent my year in Italy influenced my work and I wrote: "The influence of my work after a year's residence in Italy cannot be obviously noted. However, I know that the opportunity to live among some of the greatest architecture, sculpture and painting of the western world, art which proclaims and reflects man at his noblest, lifted and sharpened my aesthetic standards." The language is a little high flown but nevertheless true. For a young American art student to live for a year in a country like Italy, which is like living in a museum without walls, a country of beautiful cities, great architecture, paintings, a rich tradition of beauty stretching back into history for hundreds of years, was on the one hand inspiring and on the other hand sobering in that it provided a larger perspective from which to observe the art of one's own time and one's own community.

And speaking of community, on the boat on my way to Italy there was an artist who I had known when I was a student at Columbia—He was a member of a cooperative gallery on East Tenth Street in New York and he suggested that when I returned from Italy that I bring my work around, that maybe the members would ask me to join the gallery. His name was Charles Cajori and the gallery was called the Tanager. So in 1953 I returned to New York, found an apartment, showed my work to the members of the Tanager, was accepted and became a member. I could go on and on about the Tanager Gallery but let me just say that from 1952-1962 it showed the work of over two hundred young and old artists most of whom were without an uptown gallery and all of whom we felt deserved a space in which their work could be viewed by the public. We made very few sales, but the critics came, the artists came and the general public came and quite a few of the artists established themselves uptown in good galleries and had successful careers. Three that you all may have heard of were Bill King, Philip Pearlstein and Alex Katz and—oh yes, Tom Wesselman.

New York was a very exciting place to be in the 50's and 60's. The dominant figures in my corner of the New York scene were Jackson Pollock, Franz Kline, De Kooning, Rothko, Philip Guston and Ad Reinhardt— all of them abstract artists but on the fringe of this group and very much respected, even though a figurative artist, was Fairfield

Porter. These were the artists whose work we talked about and rushed to see when they had an exhibition. It was a very dynamic period particularly for painting and there was a real sense of community.

It was about this time that I began to make a shift from expressionism to a more formal or classical approach. By classical I mean a tradition of art that is moved along by the magnetic pull of a sensed ideal condition beyond the personality of the artist and beyond the turmoil that surrounds us. This approach which I call classical is expressed in terms of symmetry and a kind of restrained detachment.

At this time in New York I saw the work of Philip Guston and Ad Reinhardt. This would be around 1954. Guston was painting those lovely lyrical abstract paintings which are reminiscent of late Monets and seemed to generally link up with the French Impressionists in terms of color, paint quality and brush strokes. I also liked the fact that he emphatically placed the image in the center of the canvas. Ad Reinhardt was a different matter. He was ruthless in eliminating almost all physical, tactile, ingratiating means available to the artist. He was the dark monk of the New York art scene. When he went into his studio he seemed to get rid of almost everything. He, in a sense, you could say he fasted. His paintings were low-keyed, austere, spare and ungiving. They were a sermon on restraint. Seen from a distance they appeared to be monochromatic but when one drew near one could see rectangles of slightly different value. After the bacchanalian orgy of paint throwing, dripping and splashing that went on in some quarters of the Lower East Side of New York, Reinhardt's astringent, restrained canvases were at times a welcome relief. I admired his multiple means of saying 'no' to so much. There was such an abundance of paintings that never rose above the level of mere ego-dripping extravaganzas.

Whatever the reasons may have been, I began to simplify my paintings. The paintings continued to be abstract and expressionistic but the number of forms became fewer and fewer. These paintings usually started with an undergrowth of expressionistic lines and colors and they were gradually painted out until only two or three forms remained and then one day the inevitability occurred – I painted out everything which left me with sort of a plain but agitated surface and nothing more. They were painted in lacquer with a wide sable brush that I bought in a hardware store. The brush was about four inches wide. The paint was laid on in thin transparent layers. The only suggestion of an image, which gradually emerged as time went on, was a slight darkening in the center. But they were pretty much monochromatic. I continued along this path for about four years not really satisfied with what I was turning out but I did have a feeling that a search to give form to a vastly reduced image could be productive and meaningful.

In 1958 the Museum of Modern Art presented an enormous retrospective exhibition of the work of Georges Seurat—lithographs, sketches, studies and paintings including the wall-sized *A Sunday Afternoon on the Island of La Grande Jatte*. I was immediately struck by his success in giving a sense of volume and energy to simple shapes. Those little points of color energized the total work. I remember in particular a painted sketch of a seated woman's back. It is a small painting maybe ten inches by eight inches. It is a sketch for a much larger painting entitled *Les Poseuses*, an interior with three female nudes, one standing, one in profile seated and the third seated with her back to the viewer. There were oil sketches for each of these three figures and they were very beautiful. I hung around these sketches like a moth around a flame and so it was after this exhibition that I began to experiment rather tentatively at first with a somewhat pointillist technique, abandoning the wide sable brush, continuing in a monochromatic approach but applying the paint in little touches with a small bristle brush. Later, my palette was enlarged in terms of color.

In the 1960's my paintings had a dark center. I think I felt that the core should have weight, that the center needed to be anchored down. One day a friend, the painter Lois Dodd, visited my studio and wondered if I had ever painted a picture which was light in the center. It seemed like a good idea so I began to experiment with a light in the center. I began to experiment with a light center and it gradually became, not a matter of anchoring but of searching for a kind of radiance.

In a way I think of myself as an illustrator, in fact, I think that all art is essentially illustration. We don't create anything if you think about it for a minute we just re-combine what nature and life present us with. So, as I said at the beginning, for about thirty years I have traveled this rather narrow path of the picture as the total image and I suppose it should really be for others to say what they are all about, but if someone should come up to me and say that when they look at them they feel warmed, refreshed and at peace...
I would be very happy.

Exhibited Works

Previous Page: Detail of *Untitled (Gold Leaf)*, 2010, Oil on Canvas, 24″ x 24″, ©Sally Hazelet Drummond, courtesy Alexandre Gallery, New York

Exhibited Works

The following are a list of works included in the exhibition **Iconoclastic Fervor: Sally Hazelet Drummond's Road to Abstraction** *held at the Hite Art Institute November 19th- December 18th, 2015.*

Girl Sitting
ca.1940
Oil on Masonite
24" x 20"
Collection of Mr. and Mrs. John H. Clark IV

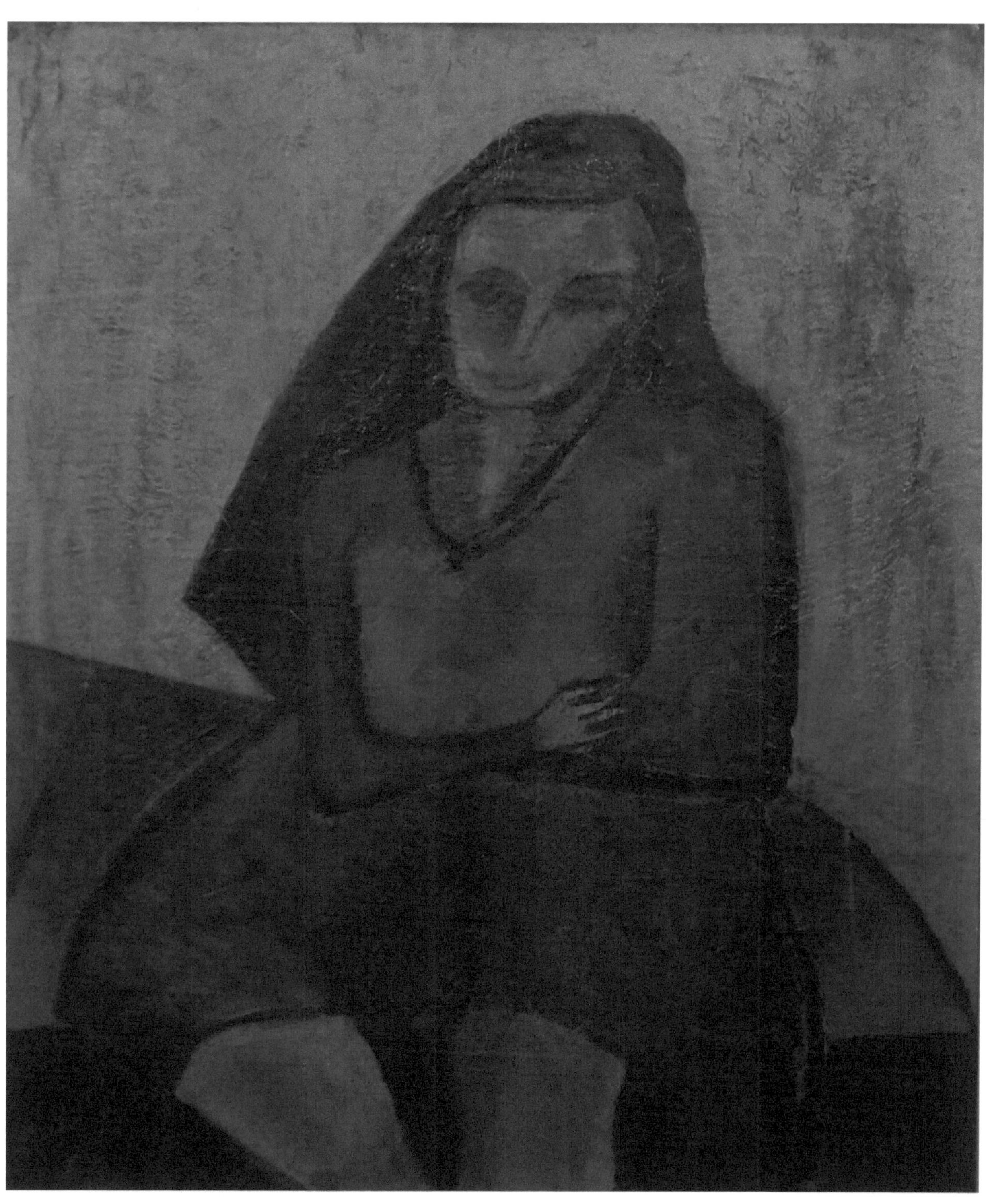

Girl in a Doorway
1949
Oil on Canvas
24" x 18"
Collection of the Artist

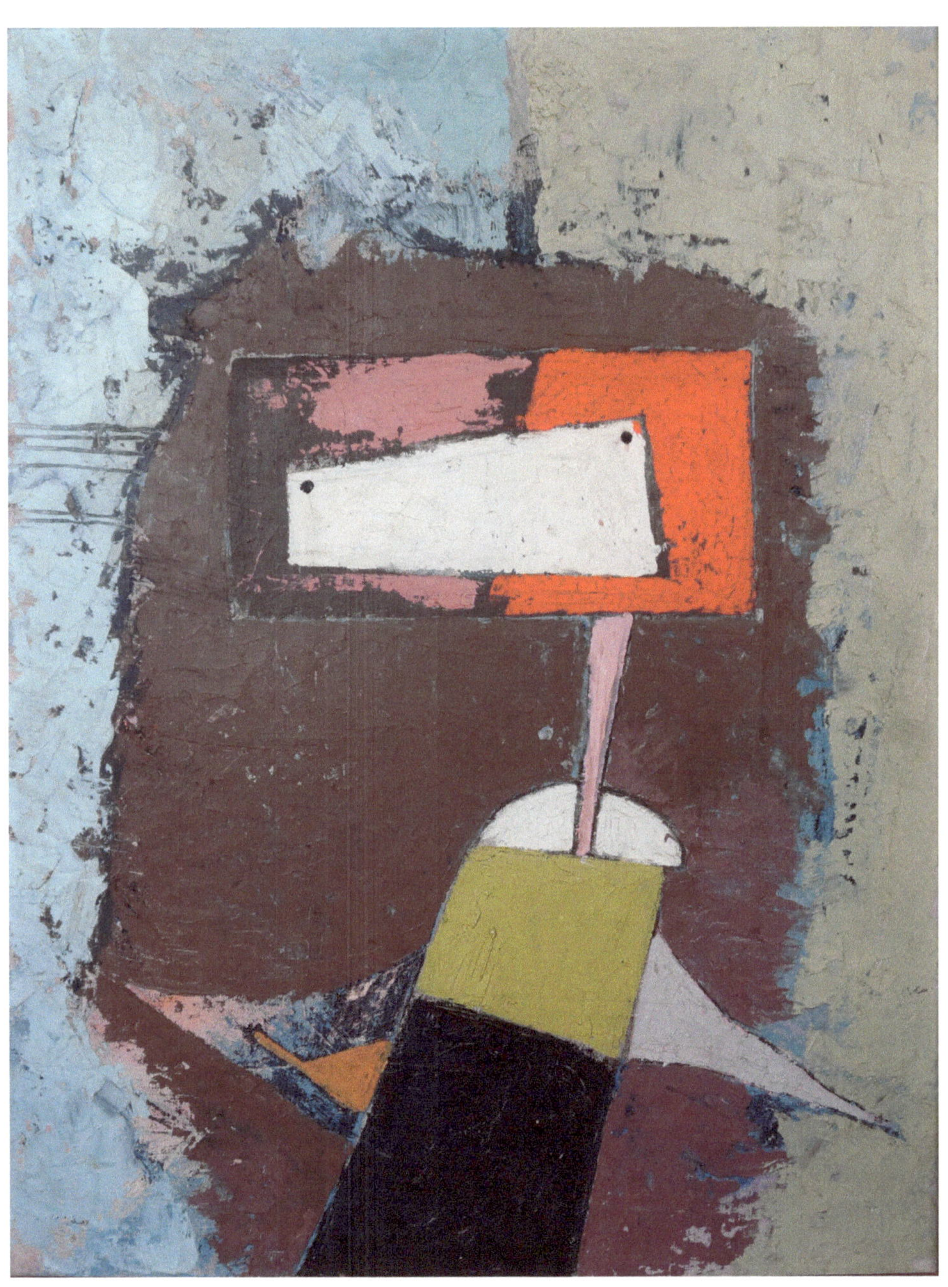

Magician
1951
Lacquer on Gessoed Masonite
48" x 32"
Collection of the Artist

____

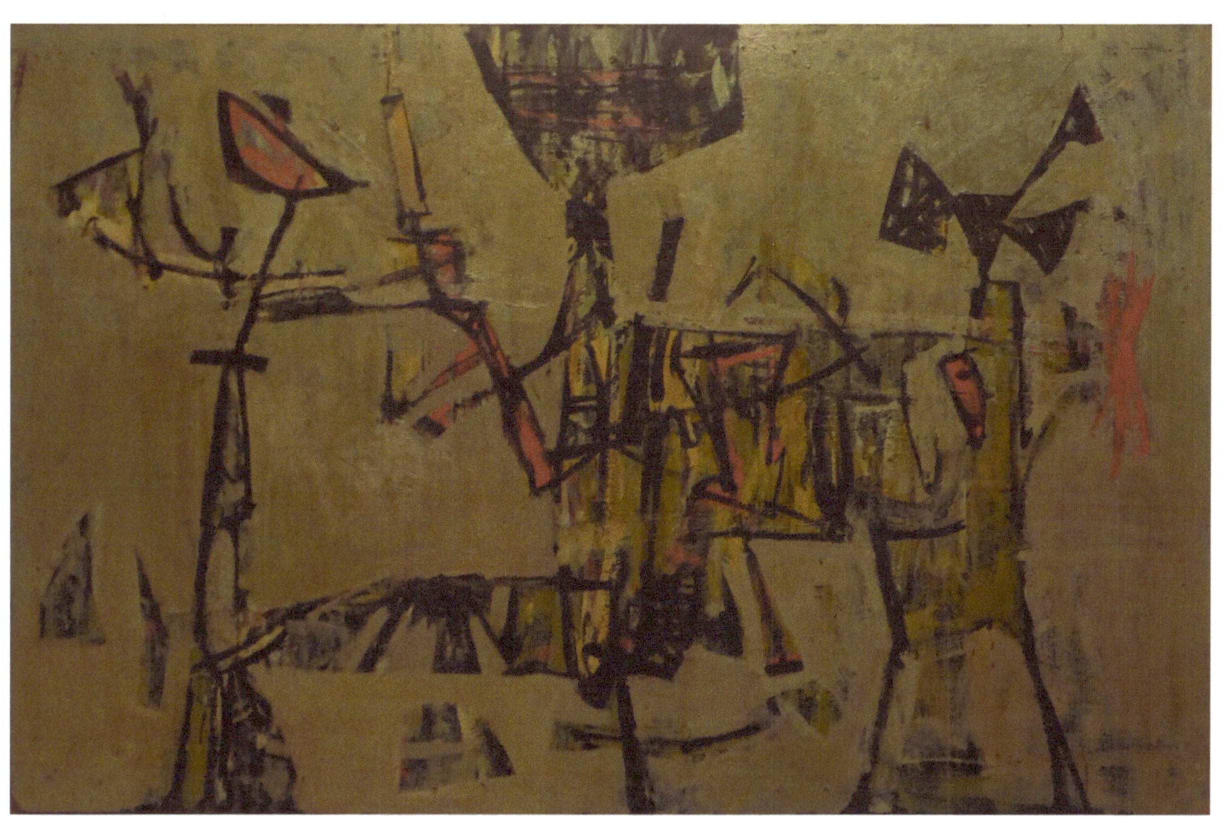

Untitled
ca. 1952
Lacquer on Gessoed Masonite
35 ½" x 24"
Collection of the Artist

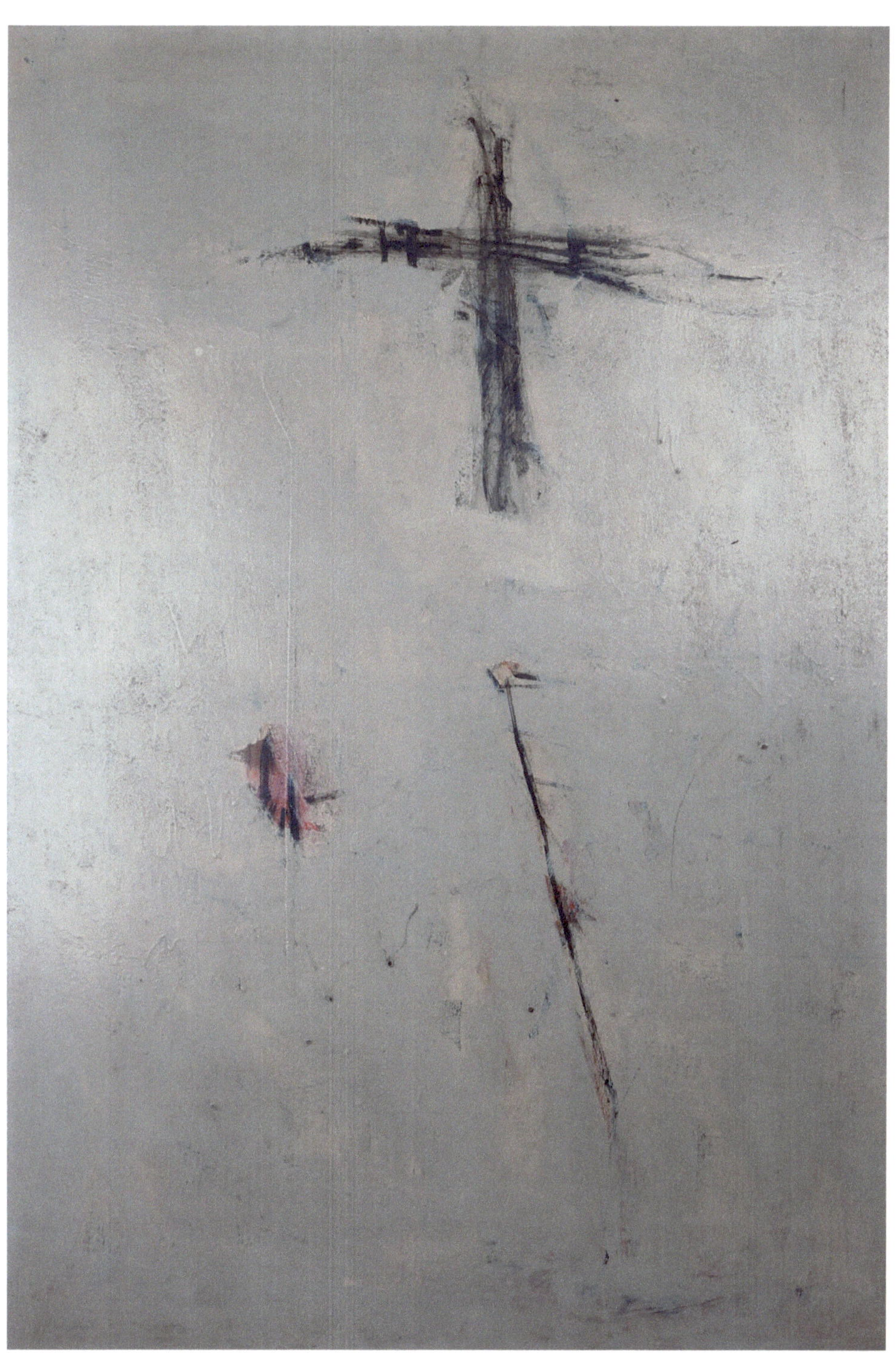

Bluebird
1960
Oil on Canvas
24" x 24"
Alexandre Gallery

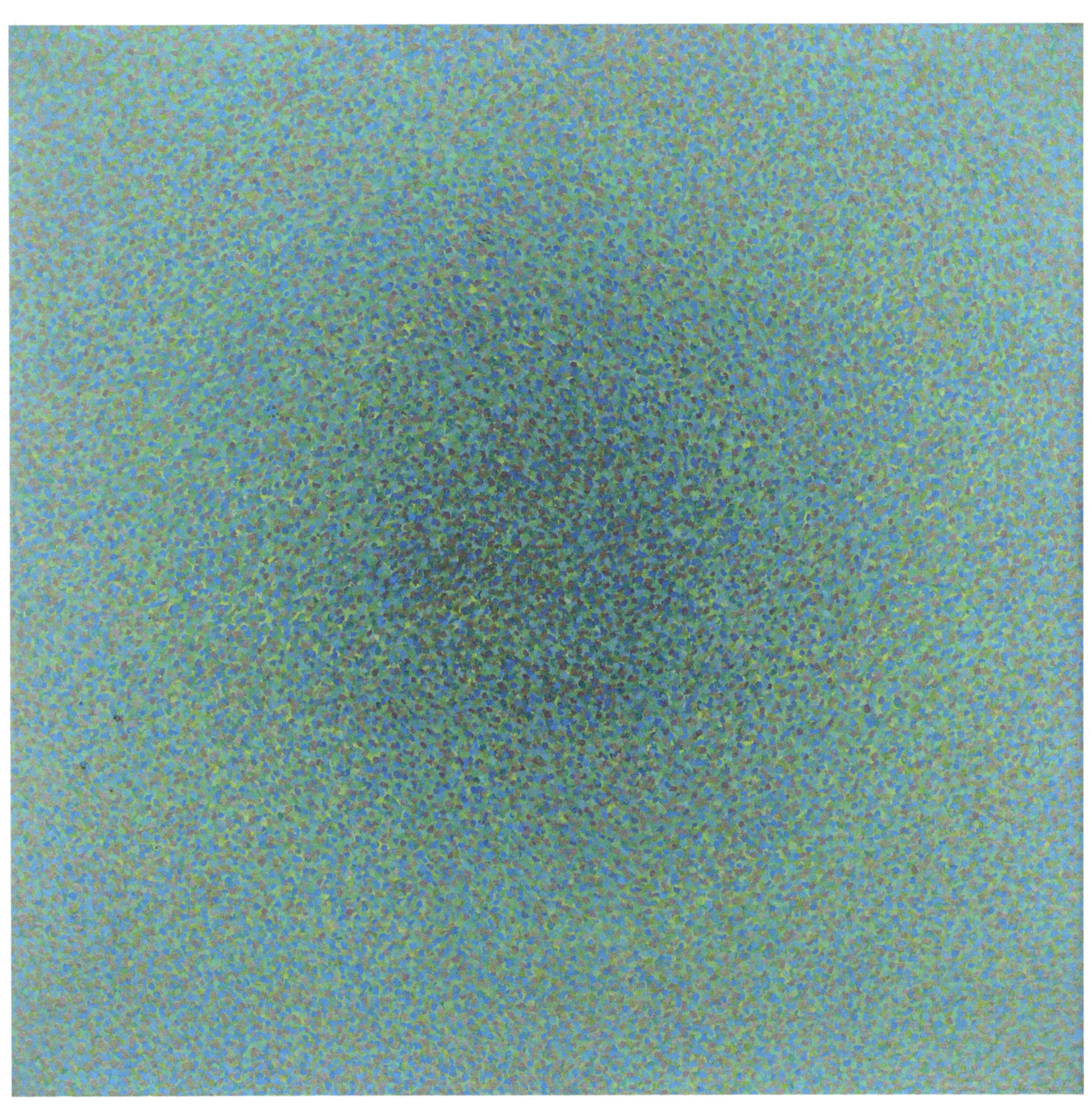

Heart of Iron
ca. 1960
Oil on Canvas
60" x 60"
Alexandre Gallery

A Simple Arrangement
1969
Oil on Canvas
18" x 18"
Collection of Mr. and Mrs. John H. Clark IV

Union Place
1978
Oil on Canvas
40" x 40"
Alexandre Gallery

———————————————

Night Flight
1978
Oil on Canvas
50" x 50"
University of Louisville Hite Art Institute

Unified Field
1980
Oil on Canvas
30" x 30"
Alexandre Gallery

Daisy Newman
1984-1985
Oil on Canvas
46" x 46"
Alexandre Gallery

No Separation
1991
Oil on Canvas
36" x 36"
Alexandre Gallery

Untitled (Gold Leaf)
2010
Oil on Canvas
24" x 24"
Alexandre Gallery

Sally Hazelet Drummond

Born: 1924, Evanston, Illinois

Education

Rollins College, 1942-44
Columbia University, B.S. 1948
Institute of Design, Chicago 1950
University of Louisville, M.A. 1952

Grants

Fulbright, Venice 1952-1953
Guggenheim Fellowship,
    Lacoste 1967-68

One-Person Exhibitions

2015   Hite Art Institute, Louisville, KY
2005   Alexandre Gallery, New York, NY
2000   Mitchell Algus Gallery, New
        York,NY
1990   Louisville Visual Arts Association,
        Louisville, KY
1989   The Cornell Fine Arts Center,
        Rollins College, Winter Park, FL
1984   Artists Space, sponsored by
        the Mark Rothko Foundation,
        New York, NY
1981   The Aldrich Museum,
        Ridgefield, CT
1978   Fischbach Gallery, New York, NY
1972   Corcoran Gallery of Art,
        Washington, D.C. *Retrospective*
1968   Fischbach Gallery, New York, NY
1962   Green Gallery, New York, NY
1960   Tanager Gallery, New York, NY
1957   Tanager Gallery, New York, NY
1952   Hadley Gallery, Louisville, KY

Selected Group Exhibitions

2007   *Invitational Exhibition of
        Contemporary Art*, American
        Academy of Arts and Letters, Jimmy
        Ernst Award in Art, New York, NY
        *Optic Nerve- Perceptual Art from the
        1960s*, Columbus Museum of Art,
        Columbus, OH
2001   The Armory Show, New York, NY
2000   National Academy of Design, 175th
        Annual Exhibition, New York, NY
1995   Artist's Choice – Elizabeth Murray,
        Museum of Modern Art,
        New York, NY
1994   5 Points Gallery, East Chatham, NY
1987   Owensboro Museum of Fine Art,
        Owensboro, KY
        National Arts Club, New York, NY
1984   *Underknown*, curated by Henry
        Geldzahler, P.S. 1, New York, NY
1983   *Abstract Paintings of the 1960s*, P.S. 1,
        New York, NY
1982   Speicher and Hassam Fund
        Exhibition, American Academy of
        Arts and Letters
1977   *Point*, Philadelphia College of Art,
        Philadelphia, PA
        Connecticut Artists, University of
        Bridgeport, Bridgeport, CT
        *10th Street Days: The Co-ops of the
        1950s*, Pleiades Gallery,
        New York, NY
1975   *A Change of View*, Aldrich Museum,
        Ridgefield, CT
1974   *Focus-Women's Work: American Art*,
        Philadelphia, PA American Academy
        of Arts